I0157053

WATTAYA MEAN MEN DON'T CARE?

A Collection of Poetry
"Men making true confessions"

Published By
Milligan Books

Cover Design By
Kerry Denson

Formatting By
AbarCo Business Services

BY
LEWIS L. SAUNDERS

Copyright © 1998 by Lewis L. Saunders
Los Angeles, California
All rights reserved
Printed and Bound in the United States of America

Published and Distributed by:
Milligan Books
an imprint of Professional Business Consultants
1425 W. Manchester, Suite B,
Los Angeles, California 90047
(213) 750-3592

First Printing, November 1998
10 9 8 7 6 5 4 3 2 1

ISBN 1- 881524-43-4

All rights reserved. No part of this book may be reproduced in
whole or in part, in any form or by any means, electronic or
mechanical, including photocopying, recording or by any
information storage and retrieval system, without permission
in writing from the author. Address inquires to *Milligan
Books,* 1425 W. Manchester, Suite B, Los Angeles, California
90047, (323) 750-3592

Printed in the United States of America

ACKNOWLEDGEMENT

I would like to give all praise, honor and glory to my Lord and Savior, Jesus Christ. He gifted me with a peace and filled my heart with the words to tell the stories. He has brought me from a long lonely road, as only he could.

I want to thank the countless men who took a moment to share their innermost feelings and thoughts on the subjects contained within. I trust they will be happy with the results. A great big thank you goes out to my family. In particular, my mother, Leona M. Perry and my brother, Elliot Myers, for believing in me. A huge thank you and lots of love to my high school English teacher, Mrs. Elaine Stuckey, for igniting a strong desire in me to constantly read, write, and create; and she has been my "second Mom". I want to thank: my "baby sis's" Joy Epps, Patrice Haydel and Lorraine Johnson for loving, listening and caring (especially when I was hurting the most), Shannon Tanner for inspiring me to share my poetry with whoever might listen; Kerry Denson (my best friend since ninth grade!) who shared his enormous artistic talent for the cover and gave his undying and sincere support of my efforts. Thank you to my pastor, Bishop Charles E. Blake at West Angeles Church of God in Christ, for his prayers, blessings, support and guidance, as well as my brothers and sisters in the Singles Ministry and Praise

Chorale choir. Thanks to all the gang at PE and my fellow writers in the Writer's Corner. A special thanks to Veronica Abernathy and Alice Wilson for their sincere, honest and true friendships and for their never wavering faith and support. Alice contributed to the poem "Temptation of Despair".

This book is lovingly dedicated to the memory of my father, Lewis H. Saunders, who I miss profoundly. In my heart, he is and will always be the greatest man I have ever had the privilege of knowing and loving.

ls

Table of Contents

Acknowledgements   4

Preface   9
Help   11

CHAPTER I   LOVE'S LOSS   13

Temptation Of Despair   14
Love's Demise   17
Did You Hear That?   19
Just A Step   20
OL' Mr, Lonely   22
She Didn't Know   23
The Search   26
Closure?   28

CHAPTER II   LOVE'S RESOLVE   31

Wanted   32
More Often   34
Cosmosis   36
Call Me   38
Go Stop   40
Ain't Nothin' Wrong With   42
Booga' Bears Can Dance, Too!!!!   44
Would That   46
No More Rebounds   47
False Digits   48

Table of Contents

CHAPTER III   LOVE'S GOALS & PROMISE   49

I Watched You	50
Lord, How Do I Do This?	51
Date With An Angel	52
First Kiss	54
Just Ask	55
Love On A Cloud	56
Saturday Morning	58
Mirrors	60
"My Eyes"	62
Engaging	64
Now !!!!!!!!!!	66
Your Night Of Passion	68
Together, Forever, As One With God	71

Preface

Oprah, Sally, Ricki and Jerry, each at one time or another have had female guests who believe - "All men are dogs" - "Men are from some other planet" - "There aren't any good men left; all the good ones are taken." Most of talk shows have depicted the jerks and idiots out there and the women that have been hurt by them. Yes, we have all occasionally heard and read about those kinds of men. And quite frankly, ladies, just like you, there are a lot of us men who are tired of being categorized and generalized into that group.

Watching such a show, after experiencing an extremely traumatic and almost deadly end to my marriage, is what led to the writing of this book. I knew I couldn't be the only man who had gone through the emotional, mental and physical hell of abandonment or loss of love!!!!

This is a book of poetry about love and loss of love from men's point of view. The poems contained herein are about and of men who are interested in commitment, not afraid of their vulnerability, and looking for that one true love to share the rest of their lives with. Men who are strong enough in themselves to be gentle and considerate. Men who are searching for women who can appreciate these qualities and love them for who they are.

Each poem is based on an actual interview or interviews of men from a wide range of ages and ethnicity, from all walks of life and social strata. These interviews were conducted over a period of a year and a half.

There are so many emotions and stories involved that a continuous series can be done. And while this book does not pretend to tell the story of every man, hopefully it will enlighten each and every one who reads it to some truths that have been subdued, overlooked or just plain discounted.

The expression goes - " A good man is hard to find." Well, in my journey to research this book, I found a lot of good men out there. I hope you enjoy meeting them through their thoughts and emotions as much as I did.

HELP?

"It's O.K., baby, don't cry - that's
Grandma's big boy" - words said
to us as a child whenever a knee
was skinned or we bumped our heads.

We got hit by baseballs, fell off skates
as with our friends, we would play.
"Big boys don't cry" - to ease the
pain is what parents and
other relatives would say.

Pre-teen and adolescence - had a feeling
hangin' out with just the guys - somethin' missing.
"Hey man - be a man - forget girls.
What are you - some kind of a sissy"?!!!!!!

Through the years - at barber shops - on the street
big brothers, uncles and older male friends would say
"Oh man, there's plenty of women, plenty of time -
it's the whole field - that's what you should play".

Jr. high & high school - fields of battle
trying for athletic prowess to gain.
coaches, teammates push -" get tougher,
stronger - play through the pain".

Fresh into college - maybe found a special love.
Now best friends and homeboys want to school you.
"Yo' man, be the man - stay on top!!!
Don't you dare let a woman rule you!!".

11

As an adult - women seem to come and go
always seemingly on the run.
Friends advise - "Don't let on that she hurt you -
just go out and find another one".

Our mothers would see our pain
and not knowing what else to do;
say "You'll be all right, honey, she really
wasn't good enough or right for you".

Now here you stand - feelings hurt - ready to leave,
not understanding and throwing a fit!!!!!!!!!!
Because you and other women can't understand
why some men have trouble getting in touch
with and expressing their feelings;
and a harder time trying to commit.

PLEASE.......

UNDERSTAND........

BE PATIENT......

AND HELP...........

ME!!!!!!!!!

ls

Chapter I

LOVE'S LOSS

Men are told that it takes us longer to commit to a relationship. If that's true, then when we do commit, it's serious. It also follows that if we lose it, that's serious, too!! Allow yourself to understand the pain that these men describe concerning the loss of true love in their lives. Including an enlightening message from a father to his child; as well as a hum/an/imalistic description of love's loss with no closure.

TEMPTATION OF DESPAIR

Depression has become you.
What is there to do?
Yesterday.. there was love
..promise.. the future.
Today.. nothing to hold onto.
So much transformation
in so little time.

Twisted and distorted,
the face of a stranger
stares back at you
as you gaze into the
mirror to start your day.

Heartbreak has revisited;
ravaging your features & peace.
Reverting a once proud,
majestic, towering oak;
to an uprooted, weak seedling.

You struggle daily
in your surroundings
with the simplest of things;
like space and time.
Sometimes lying so still...
breathing so shallow.

Some friends rally...
bringing damage control,
trying to be compassionate?
But.. seeing no
evidence of struggle,
no open wound,
no pool of blood..
they exit....
along with understanding!!

What silent viper
has struck you down?
leaving the acrid venom of
despair, hopelessness,
anger, confusion,
self doubt, disappointment
loneliness and
old festering wounds
racing through your veins?
Numbing your mind.

Death....
smells your vulnerability,
lurking in the shadows;
teasing you with its empty promise
of no more pain.....
Yeah... no more pain!!!!

STOP!!!! it's time to resist!!!
Time to fight back!...
regain control...
don't let this illusion
take you out!!!!

Allow the
GOD GIVEN STRENGTH
you were gifted with at birth,
to remove that unwelcome
and undeserved
burden and weight.
Let it lift you to
a place of illumination,
of greater perspective,
and unlimited view
of your endless
options and choices.

Is

LOVE'S DEMISE

Emotions that churn like
an angry river.
Each day, every minute
causing gentle thoughts to differ.

Love's flow, once a torrent
reduced to a trickle.
True colors shown -
the shade..... fickle!!!

The death of love
is the test of the spirit.
So often unseen
the truth..... too near it!!!!!

Love favors switched
from pleasure to duty.
Transformed into drudgery
from a point of beauty.

Secrets of the heart
unspoken and concealed.
Confusion dies - understanding grows
if only revealed.

Where two had formed
a strong bond - now stark division.
Instead of two living as one;
only one made the decision.

Through silence and time
past love shows no regrets.
I thought she really loved me -
am I so easy to forget ???!!!!!!!

ls

DID YOU HEAR THAT?

Did you hear that?
The sound of my breaking heart
and the deafening sound of loneliness
now that she's no longer here.

Love's fantasies - gone - all taken flight
Cold - replaces warmth - into each night.

Soft tender footsteps gone out the door;
her joyous laughter tickles my ears no more.

Candlelit baths, moonlit walks,
whispering in her ear;
I'd give all I own just to have her near.

Pearls of sadness in my eyes - shimmering;
the sweet taste of her lips - now just a memory.

End of work - anticipated, magic time of day;
homeward bound and with her - time to play.

Love's unfortunate mistakes - forever to regret;
unconditional devotion - so easy to forget??!!

Did you hear that?
The sound of my breaking heart
and the deafening sound of loneliness
now that she's no longer here.

Is

JUST A STEP......

You couldn't believe
that I loved you
any more than I could
tell you what to do.
Go figure........
Just because I married
your mother - did I think
love and respect were due?

You were never
my responsibility;
that duty fell on
your Mom and Dad.
It was my personal choice
to bring to your life
and show you things
that they never had.

But, you made it clear -
my job was just to supply
your material needs,
while my desire to feel some
gratitude was not something
you intended to heed.

I knew your nonchalance
resulted from a missing
father not seeming to care.
That challenged me to
work harder at being supportive,
just trying to be there.

It never occurred to you that
in providing for you
in our house.
I sometimes shortchanged
my own flesh and blood
taking time from their time
food from their mouths.

My birthday,
Christmas, Father's day
from you to me -
not special events.
No emotions shared -
no thoughts presented;
and with that I should be content?

Sadly, I realized upon intense
reflection and after it
was all said and done;
that you were simply mirroring
what your mother had begun.

Never tried to be your parent
Hoped to be a respected friend.
Knowing full well that
if your mother ever left me
- our relationship would end.

And one day....... she did ..... and it did!!!!!!

ls

OL' MR. LONELY

Ol' Mr. Lonely.....
my ultimate fear
and long an enemy.
No matter which way I turn
around the corner you've
always been.

Thought for sure this time forever
I had defeated you -
old powerful foe.
Had no idea she
had become your ally;
how could I know?

You're a terrible feeling - Ol Mr. Lonely;
the thought of you
ruins many a day.
Hope does not spring eternal
once you have had your way.

With the hearts and souls
you already have
hanging under your umbrella;
you could have walked on by,
you didn't have
to claim this fella.
But, since you're here
in your usual manner -
you don't leave unless you win.
Move on over
all the rest of you
I might as well settle on in.

ls

SHE DIDN'T KNOW......

Your mama didn't know so ....
she couldn't tell you ....
that watching you
leave, took my breath away;
leaving behind a black
hole where emotions once dwelled.

That I missed your
tiny footsteps
around the house;
the sweetness of your
joy as you were at play.
Your big beautiful eyes
searching mine for
protection and love;
your little hand
enclosed in mine
as we walked together.

She didn't know so ......
she couldn't tell you ....
That court-ordered
once-in-a-while visits
hurt almost as much
as never seeing you.

That time spent visiting
was time for reintroduction,
time catching up
on missed moments,
and time eating away at
shared, present thoughts
as well as future dreams.

She didn't know so ...
she couldn't tell you .....
That the pain of sending
support payments
is not in the sending;
but in never seeing the
results of may labor.

The pain of
not seeing the excitement
in your eyes,
not hearing your squeals
of delight,
not feeling your little arms
around my neck,
not hearing "thank you, daddy"
when it's
fresh and new.

She didn't know so ...
she couldn't tell you ......
That through the years
most of my quiet thoughts
were of you and longing for
our closeness.

That sometimes my silence
and/or absence was to protect you from
my tears;
and to not see you
as happy without me
as you once were with me.

She didn't know so ......
she couldn't tell you ....
That through it all
I shout to the world
about the pride, joy
and privilege of being
your father.

That I still long
for our closeness and
that I love you so
much more than
you will ever know.

Is

THE SEARCH

My eyes still search for you:
in the sea of faces
as I walk on any street.
in each car I pass
no matter who is in it.

each time I wake up
in our bed - still empty and cold.
in the living room
listening to music - dancing/singing.

in the stores where we shopped
with you perusing all the aisles.
in the seat next to me
as I travel to and fro.

in the kitchen... where
your special flavor was welcome.
in the bathtub with bubbles
where a peek brought a smile.

in some sexy lingerie
with that cute sheepish grin.
in my corner..
loving me - helping me win.

But my eyes realize, sadly;
the only place to search for you now:
the only place where you will be found,
is in my heart , with all the memories
forever locked in my mind.

ls

CLOSURE

We mated. lived, loved
and one day you just left.
Now I feel empty.
So I prowl around.
My head is low, the sun is setting and...
(sniff, sniff)

I'm losing your scent.
It hurts... yet...
where do I lick to ease the pain?!

You used to roam my territory with me.
Now you don't even call out
as you pass by.
You've left your scent
it's like no other.....
Where do I lick to ease the pain?!

My cubs have grown and gone;
you shared them with me.
But.... I'm strong.....Oh Yes!!!!

He who sits in his tree.
He who longs for a love .....
so unattainable?!

I want the rain again...
I want the wind strong and fierce!!
(sniff, sniff)

There! I picked up your scent,
but only faintly.

My cries in the night have brought only
those who seek to hurt me...
those who I don't want to hunt wit` me

They can never find me
although they see me.
I've paced the water's edge.
I laid down next to it
and made love to the sun.
You know, I even ate the plant
that tranquilizes my muscles,
numbs my mind.

You.. you hunt in a new
part of the land...
but you still pick up my scent.

Did you forget the I know these things?
Did you forget that I sense where you are?

What made you think it wouldn't hurt me?
What made you think I would not care?
Have you become deaf to my stalking wariness?

Didn't you know it was only you
that I wanted to share
my giant limb with;
to be framed together
in the moonlight?

So I climb to the top
of my giant tree.
I cry.. I scream... I ache...
I grooooowwwwllll
for you!!!!

I know I frightened
every creature in hearing
distance.... but, it's OK.

So.. you go your way.
Roam other forests,
leaving your scent on others
as I know you will.

I will stay here on my limb
all alone again.
how cruel!!
how human!!

I don't feel like eating.
I don't feel like purring.
Just long, black, sinewy
muscles glistening,
large white fangs bared;
yellow-green eyes staring
into nothingness...............

ls

Chapter II

LOVE'S
RESOLVE

During and after a breakup, most of us resolve to do different next time. But, so many crawl inside of ourselves, hide our hearts and try to think of methods to avoid the pain in the future. Others get into some deep introspective searching; and still others used that time to make and solidify boundaries to be implemented in relation to the manner that women view and interact with them in the human dance called dating and relationships. For so many, a breakup lends an opportunity to regain ourselves.

<u>WANTED?</u>

I hear Christian women say-
Wanted:
a God-loving, honest, sensitive,
passionate, hardworking man,
one who wants <u>one</u> real love
& one unafraid of commitment.

So I come unto you full of honesty,
with my heart in my hand.
Going to work everyday
and loving God in every way.

My search is very similar
in nature and purpose to yours.
I'm about receiving and giving
and cherish the simple joys of living.

My commitment is in serving
the Lord; and my passion,
is in doing his will.
Without HIM, your ultimate
mate satisfaction I can not fulfill.

I, too look forward to
the simple joys like:
-the holding of hands-
-long walks on the beach-
-cuddling over the phone-
-regular full body hugs-
-breakfasts in bed-
Valentine's Day wishes.

I look forward to sharing:
-the Sunday funnies-
-trials and tribulations-
-ribbons of early morning sunlight-
-the giggling times and the crying ones, too-
-lots of bubbles in a shower or bath....oooh!!!!!!

BUT MOST IMPORTANT.....
growing in Christ, our Lord & Savior.

But....... I don't have a washboard stomach
nor a car you can describe
with less than five letters.
I don't look like Denzel
or dress in Armani
I don't come anywhere close
to six figure money.

So....... you look at me and say:
"You're not my type"
and move on to wait for the
man described above;
Not stopping to realize
that if you had seen my heart
you may have received your
heaven-sent, forever love.

ls

MORE OFTEN........

Aside from the immediate family;
more often than not, the person or persons
who cry the hardest at funerals
let opportunities to share love
or an important thought pass them by.

Like Rip Van Winkle -
time seems to have passed some by.
Societal rules & emotional games
have replaced honesty and innocence
in the human dance called
mating - man and woman.

One hears:
"Don 't let on that you like them, until they do first"
"Let some time pass before you call"
"Don't you think you're moving too fast?"

Secrets of the heart become lies -
disguised as "protecting oneself";
imbedded in the hearts of those
who seek the truth and claim to give it.

What direction?
Have faith in God's saving grace,
remain true to oneself;
take the time to share
like or love while it's fresh
and innocent. Because...........

Aside from the immediate family;
more often than not, the person or persons
who cry the hardest at funerals
let opportunities to share love
or an important thought pass them by.

ls

<u>COSMOSIS</u>

Ladies.......
Cosmopolitan magazine is just a
bunch of papers bound together
and most other women's
magazines too.
But they seem to have become
the final word in providing
information on men
to most of you.

They entertain and seduce
you with success story,
mannequin, model types.
Making everyday men get lost
in the shuffle
after all that hype.

You take the tests
to rate your relationships
and your men.
They manipulate & guide you
on what to do with them; how,
why and when.

All manner of media
has you looking for
'their perfection' in all you do.
But, how can you expect
or look for something in others
that isn't even in you?

So, mute and wipe out that
media data bank,
set your mind
and your heart free.
Let's sit down & talk;
looking at each other,
RELATING..............
Just you and me.

ls

CALL ME?

REMEMBER HOW:
She lit a fire inside you right
from the first glance,
This classic beauty with
a peaceful confidence
had you in a trance.

But, you already had your
evening's bounty of phone numbers
that you may or may not call;
you didn't need this one;
for one night, you already had it all.

It wasn't satisfaction or insecurity that
stopped you from drawing close.
No, that wasn't the case.
You realized you had
to set your heart right
before you stepped
up to her face.

She was something unique.
Nothing like the ones
you had so easily conquered before.
She wore a peace that surpassed
all understanding and it kept
you glued to the floor.

Masking your "Mack";
when you finally spoke,
talking and sharing was easy;
like peaceful slumber.
And although she
wouldn't give you hers;
she took your
phone number.

That got to your ego
and your "Mack Daddy" ways
came into full view.
She was only
momentarily confused,
then realize -
this must be the
real you.

You exited clumsily;
realizing in your heart
that she truly
could be "the one".
wishing that your
"Mack Daddy" ego had
left you alone.

The phone has rung many
time since - but hasn't brought
the call you wanted it to.
But the 'no call' has made you
remember all the promised
calls you didn't make
or even intend to.

ls

GO.......STOP?!

YELLOW LIGHT..........
Secret glances,
like buried treasure
never discovered;
seeing the beauty of her spirit,
feelings uncovered.

Fear of rejection - shyness
were easily conquered.
I heard "yes"
to a lunch invitation.
What a wonderful word!!!!!

GREEN LIGHT.............
Lunch in a restaurant
away from curious eyes.
Looking into hers - holding
back hopeful sighs.

Minutes, hours, days -
time together
seemed so few.
But, fulfillment -
sharing thoughts,
fears, secrets -
points of view.

Coffee, a few words
in the mornings,
cuddling phone calls
at night.
Bringing to my life
a new order...
Everything's all right!!!!!!!

RED LIGHT.............
Now, she says
"pull back some
let's slow down -
give this some room."
My heart sinks -
Hope it's not
the 'second thought' -
a sign of doom.

Because her God-given
beauty and smile
I've become addicted to.
While her innocence
and honesty
I've given into.

It is said
the greatest treasures
are found
after a number of years.
So I'll sit back -
try to be patient
and let time
take care of my fears.

ls

AIN'T NOTHIN' WRONG WITH

Ain't nothin' wrong with...
showing the world that you're
proud to be with her
and happy to share her love
everyday - 24/7.

Simply by.......
holding her hand as you
walk through a crowd.
That says she's with me
says it out loud!!!!!

Or occasionally.....
pull her close &
hug her tight - just as you
hang around.
Let's everyone else know
that between you,
true love abounds.

Surprise her....
kiss the top of her head
or nuzzle the nape of her neck
as you stand in line.
Listen up fells,
this one makes her feel fine.

Relaxing at home...
cuddling & rocking her,
whispering "I love you"
from time to time.
A special, cozy way of
keeping love sublime.

Ain't nothin' wrong with...
letting her know that
she's your one and only star.
Done consistently and sincerely,
your love will go far .

Ain't nothin' wrong with....
showing the world you're
proud to be with her;
but only if it's true.
The beauty of it is-
the more you do this -
it all comes back to you......
FOR FOREVER!!!!!!!!!!!!

ls

Booga Bears Can Dance, Too!

I think you misunderstood,
I only came over to ask you to dance.
The way you just looked me over;
you must have thought I said
"want romance?"

I have no problem with a quick
"No, thank you "a pleasant refusal.
But, it becomes something else
after an up, down & all over perusal.

Your attitude says "booga' bear"
there's something about me you don't approve.
But what's the way I'm dressed or
look like got to
do with my dance moves?????

You say that's what you do
to ensure your protection.
Stop!!! put yourself in men's
shoes, we're the ones who have
to deal with this rejection!

To ask you to dance after
picking you out should
be viewed as a compliment.
Not an opportunity to make
yourself feel better
by issuing torment.

And if after one dance-
I don't get the message-
"no connection - out of
my face".
That's the time to
politely put me on any
other man in our place.

Now if you are here to
find your soul mate-
that forever lover.

Remember .... he has to be
experienced like a good
book - inside out - cover
to cover.

So, I'll leave you to look -
your Mr. Perfect to find.
The only lesson you may learn
is you are a legend
only in your mind.

And when you get back to
the real world and
all that is true.

Remember .... Picky Lady
We Booga' Bears can
dance too !!!!!!!!

WOULD THAT........

Would that one
could have been
more beautiful, more handsome
or even been taller.
More intelligent, less serious;
or even that one
should be smaller.
Listening to another's likes,
desires & expectations
can sometimes bring self-doubt.
But believing that God
makes no mistakes;
while hope is dashed,
Self-depreciation is thrown out.
Patterns of desired "types"
developed over time
resulted in relationships of brevity.
Finding the "true heart"
amidst the seeming incompatibility
could bring one blissful longevity.
But...........
some find comfort in
continuing the patterns
that lead to unnecessary
and sometimes abject loneliness.

ls

NO MORE REBOUNDS

The basketball caromed off
the backboard,
large hands snatched
it midair,
leading to a long pass,
resulting in a score.
Your heart bounced
off the backboard
of your last
relationship -
you seized it and
brought it into my court.
We played the game often.
But, just when my heart
was ready for overtime -
From nowhere -?
He captured the rebound,
scored, and you were gone.
game over.
No more recent rebounds.
my name ain't Rodman!

ls

False Digits

An evening of discovery
included glimpses of hope,
prompted by shared values,
thoughts and ideals;
due to intermittent
impromptu interviews,
interrupted by occasional
trips to the dance floor,
intensified by hard rhythms
exploding on air;
caused various interpretive,
sometimes sensual, melodic gyrations;
which enhanced the totality
of your beautiful womanhood;
that excited the totality
of my interested manhood.
Having subdued
my fear of rejection,
I vocalized a desire
for future contact
& received your seven digits.
YES!!!!!!!!!
Sincere effort and honest exchange
were unfortunately rewarded
with
FALSE DIGITS!!!!!!!!
Thereby... Making you
a contributor to
the continuous chasm
of trust and communication
between men and women.

ls

Chapter III
LOVE'S
GOALS
&
PROMISE

These men have definite goals and ideals to aspire to and achieve in their quest for that one special lady that has the ability and desire to appreciate them as they are and still love them or love them so much more because of who they truly are. Ultimately anticipating not having to play that dating game anymore and settling down as two together forever as one with God.

I WATCHED YOU

I watched you
running fluidly.....
hair flowing -
framing your pretty face.
sun kissed skin.....
surrounding
determined eyes....
beautiful, silent,
focused, and searching.
graceful neck....
laden with tiny pearls of sweat.
pert smallish breasts.....
with excited nipples
from the strain.
perfect buttocks....
sway and roll -
so wonderfully sensual!!!!!
sculpted, firm legs....
measuring every stride.

I watched you every day.
And in every way
I fell in love
with you
from a distance!!!!!!!!

ls

LORD, HOW DO I DO THIS?

All right!!! lookee there.....
nice smile - nice eyes ..all by herself - but.......
now we're entering the sanctuary..
So.... put away all thoughts except..... God!
Great service! There she goes again!
Uh oh!!! What if she's a visitor?
Lord, how do I do this??

A Friday social and .....
Ooooeee!!! God must be smilin' on me!!!!!
Hello!!! There she is again.....
Pretty eyes... She looks great in those jeans.
Thank you, God, for name tags
and intro games!!!!!!!!
She seems very nice....
Should I ask for her number now?
Lord , how do I do this ???? and when??

A Saturday outdoor concert.
Yep!!!! Fabulous smile and gorgeous!!!!!
There she is one more 'gain!!
Let's see... Run into her at Christian events
Dress looks nice on her...
Oops, was that just a lust? No way!!!!

Early... from a distance
a casual wave and slight recognition.
Later.. Up close
a handshake & friendly "A" hug.
But... now she's leaving!!!! Now!!!!!!
Lord, how do I do this?????

O. K......... Would you mind if I call you sometime?
She smiled and replied "What are you going to call me"
as she wrote her number down.
Like I said, Lord......... nothing to it!!!!!!!!!!!!!

ls

Date With An Angel

I met an angel last night
and she set my heart free.

She glided through a throng
of invisible people; her spirit
shining so brightly, lifting mine
to dizzying heights.

I met a wide-eyed angel
who searched
my soul and with a sweet
dimpled smile took away
pain and apprehension.

A gospel and music filled evening
ensued; made more precious
and heavenly by having
this mocha maiden at
my side.

Glorious satisfaction and
appreciation registered on her
face as nature's bounty -
colorful spring floral bouquet
were presented for her pleasure.

Secrets of the heart
spoken, read and exchanged,
communication effortless -
as promises of swinging on
swings and dancing on the wind
became springboards to a tomorrow.

Too soon my angel announced
her impending departure;
exciting as gracefully as
she had entered my world.
Taking with her the fragrant
bouquet and forever music
and blindly carrying
my fledgling affection
and sincere gratitude.

Ah, but time is fleeting
my evening of rapture
had to come to an end.
Yes ..... I had had a date
with an angel.
But now my gorgeous angel
is my beautiful friend.

ls

FIRST KISS

A first
kiss is
at once...
cautious,
emotional,
clumsy
wapm,
ticklish,
breathless,
sloppy,
fervent,
wet,
tingly,
urgent,
fiery,
quivery,
passionate.....
and sometimes full
of the promise and hope
of many more
and
a
real
true
love!!!!!!!
Is

JUST ASK

Oblivious to you,
out of the corner of my eye,
I notice
you studying me.
Probing my eyes,
searching my life force;
hunting for
answers to questions
you never ask.
If you want to know .....
If you need to know......
Just ask!!!!!
Our relationship is built on
truth. And truth is
strength.
We are strong enough
in ourselves and each other
to not have to ask
our friends and family.
I love you.
I'm here for us.
So...... please........
JUST ASK ME.

ls

LOVE ON A CLOUD

Inexperience and
a genuine good heart
make her unnecessarily love-shy.
This time she wants
the truth in love;
so, hello to the future -
to the past good-bye.

Her new feelings
are scattered,
most are held within.
With each taste
of her sweet soft lips;
nervousness, you transcend.

She relents,
enters your arms;
and that's when you realize
the incredible passion
suppressed behind those
fawn-like brown eyes.

She strokes you
all over softly
and moves with you the same.
Goosebumps visit,
as with pure pleasure,
you whisper her name.

Her skin,
so soft and silky,
to the lips
and to the touch.

You work so hard
for her total satisfaction
which you know
she needs so much.

The fire increases,
riding waves of ecstasy -
suspended in air.
Two souls
entwined in love's tryst -
floating, without a care.

When the sweet love has peaked,
both bodies
satiated and spent;
her long, deep moan
lets you know
what your tenderness,
strength and true love has meant.

ls

SATURDAY MORNING

Sunlight plays hide-n-seek
through the blinds
as I struggle to open my eyes
to a new day's dawning.

There's a peaceful silence
and a fuzzy warmth
being under the covers,
as a long, lazy yawn overcomes me.

My body convulses as it demands
a spine & toe curling streeeetch;
and my hand grazes your body,
causing you to stir.

I edge closer to your warmth,
only slightly hearing your gentle breathing;
trying hard not to interrupt
your peaceful slumber.

A familiar electricity charges me
as our bodies make full contact.
Still deep in sleep,
on reflex, you reach for me.

A sigh of contentment escapes from within
as I study your resting form beside me.
I gently nuzzle your neck
and a knowing smile is heard in your sigh.

My pulse quickens and my smile broadens
as I realize - - It's Saturday!!!!!!
I cuddle you more protectively
and drift back to sleep with you
It's Saturday - - we have all day!!!!!!!!!

ls

MIRRORS

*What did your mirror reflect
as you started your day?*

*Did it reflect
your motherhood warmth;
that's like fresh baked
chocolate chip cookies
on a fall day?
and the kitten-like
playfulness that bursts
forth in your giggle?*

*Did it reflect
your pretty, saucy eyes;
windows to your heart,
so full of
sincerity and integrity;
and the arch of your eyebrow
that signals introspection;
and the wide eyed excitement
of everyday rediscovery?*

*Did it reflect
your flawless skin
like a smooth, flowing river of
the sweetest melted Carmel;
and the wonderful "S" curve
frame that it clings to;
which brings
some men to fantasy....
some women to envy?*

Did it reflect
the strong willed woman
walking proud every day
while wearing so many hats;
who hasn't lost touch with
the little girl inside
that is so full of hope
for a better day and
a better way for her own?

But, most of all......
did your mirror reflect
your quiet sexuality.......
or your smoldering sensuality?
Did it reflect
how absolutely
GORGEOUS you are!?

Well, lovely lady
If it didn't...
please look into
the mirror called
"MY EYES".

ls

61

"MY EYES"

I wish you could crawl
behind my eyes
so you could see you as I do,
because again today......
you asked me "do you still love me
& am I still attractive to you?"

I look at you and think about the woman
who took a chance and accepted my
invitation for our first date.

I see you and think about all the giggles,
warmth, challenges and tears
we've shared along the way.

I gaze at you and think about the person
who grew alongside and with me
and overlooked my imperfections.

I study you and remember all your love
and support as I tried to find out
who I was and wanted to be.

I look inside you and see the strength,
tenderness, love and encouragement
that I rely on to keep forging ahead.

If you could crawl behind my eyes
and see you as I do;
you would see my eyes glaze over as I
view this magnificent, beautiful woman
who took the vow of forever with me;
who I will love, need and cherish for eternity.

Is

ENGAGING

Tears streamed, as I slipped
onto your finger, the
gold and diamond band.
A quivering "yes" issued
forth as I asked
you for your hand.

It is so wonderful to
know that you have
agreed to be my wife.
To know you love and
trust me enough
to share the rest of your life.

Every day that I have spent
with you presented
new worlds to explore.
Even with a few setbacks,
I've always wanted
and looked forward to more.

You are an incredible woman-
any man would want
you by their side.
Because you are my friend,
companion and tender love guide.

You bring balance to my life
by lovingly checking me
when I'm wrong.
While your tender spirit
and gracious heart
fill my heart with song.

With unbridled excitement,
I anticipate the day
we say "I do" or "I will".
The first day of the rest
of <u>OUR LIVES AS ONE</u>;
our loving cups
completely filled.

I LOVE YOU SO MUCH!!!!!!!

ls

NOW!!!!!!!!!!

Time was, I was lonely
even in the arms of the one I loved.
Now......My loving cup is full even
when you aren't near.

Time was, I was expected to change
me to satisfy another.
Now.....you choose to love
and accept me just as I am.

Time was, attempts to communicate
led to frustration and confusion.
Now.....it's great to be listened to,
comforted and cared about.

Time was, the sense of needing love
was a one way street.
Now.....we're needing each other and
basking in the warmth.

Time was, kindness and thoughtfulness
were taken for granted and tossed aside.
Now.....you understand and appreciate;
and find joy in the simplest of things.

Time was, the future was a stormy sea of
faces and a void in my heart.
Now.....your constant attention and tender
loving have calmed the sea and filled the void.

Time was, love didn't have a meaning,
nor did it have a name.
Now.....forever is love's meaning
and you and I.... is its name.

Now.........don't stop. Let's do this!!!!!!!!!!!!
                                                    ls

YOUR NIGHT OF PASSION

Arriving home from work;
darkness surprises and surrounds
you as you pass through
the portals of passion.
Aromatic wisps of incense
floating on air
tease your senses.

My finger to your lips
effects the required silence;
and a gentle nudge directs you
to a place of comfort
as your eyes adjust to
the dusky ambiance.

The removal of your shoes
and the ensuing spine-releasing
massage of your tired feet
triggers the initial submission.
Candles dot this ebony atmosphere;
Softly illuminating the cloud-like,
fluffy pillows underfoot.

Subdued, easy jazz embraces you
as I assist you into nakedness.
I taste the passion and gratitude
in your lips as I tenderly
lift, then transport you
to the room where I
gently lower you into
a warm liquid respite.

Your closed eyes
and appeased sighs
signal increasing surrender
as you succumb to the fragrant,
bubbly elixir which now
totally engulfs you.

This womb-like tranquillity
is suspended only
as you are hand fed
chocolate-dipped strawberries
and sips of cool wine.

In due time,
I coax you to your feet
and mildly bathe
every curve and angle
or your glistening essence;
languidly lingering
at your greater sensitivity;
initiating tingly sensations
and a further yielding.

A big, soft cotton towel
sheaths you as
I pat you dry;
while the shadow
of candlelight dances
across your dripping
wet, sweet form.

I gingerly introduce
your now listless frame to
a bed of pillows;
thoroughly caress you
with heated oil, and feel your
muscles relinquish
their last vestige of control.

I gather you up in my arms,
feel the goosebumps
visiting your skin;
draw you into my chest;
and cover us with
a warm blanket.

I faithfully whisper
how much I
appreciate and love you
as I rock us both to
sleep in our favorite
rocking chair.

ls

TOGETHER, FOREVER, AS ONE WITH GOD

Two Souls borne into this world through
God's tender love, mercy and forethought.
Marking their steps as a boy and a girl.
THROUGH SWEET SURRENDER!!!!
Two Souls borne unto HIS word
and borne anew *as one with God*.

Two Personalities developed through teachings
from
& relationships with parents, friends, the family
chain, casual and business contacts from babe
to adult.
THROUGH SWEET SURRENDER.....
Two Personalities enjoined and developed in
Christ,
seeking truth *as one with God*.

Two Hearts beating the contrary pulses of
hope-despair, love-hate, confidence-worry
puppy love-lust, joy-sadness....
both trying to find the balance in love.
THROUGH SWEET SURRENDER....
Two Hearts equally yoked,
filled with the blood of Jesus Christ
as one with God.

BOOK AVAILABLE THROUGH
Milligan Books
An Imprint Of Professional Business
Consulting Service

Wattaya
Mean Men Don't Care $10.95

Order Form

Milligan Books
1425 West Manchester, Suite B,
Los Angeles, California 90047
(323) 750-3592

Mail Check or Money Order to:
Milligan Books

Name _____ Date _____

Address _____

City_____ State _____ Zip Code_____

Day telephone _____

Evening telephone_____

Book title _____

Number of books ordered ___ Total cost .... $_____

Sales Taxes (CA Add 8.25%) .... $_____

Shipping & Handling $3.00 per book .... $_____

Total Amount Due..$_____

· Check   · Money Order   Other Cards _____

· Visa   · Master Card   Expiration Date _____

Credit Card No. _____

Driver's License No. _____

Signature   Date

www.ingramcontent.com/pod-product-compliance
Lightning Source LLC
Chambersburg PA
CBHW032028040426
42448CB00006B/765